WHAT'S NEXT FOR AI

CHARTING THE UNKNOWN FUTURE OF ARTIFICIAL INTELLIGENCE

by Tammy Enz

CAPSTONE PRESS
a capstone imprint

Published by Capstone Press, an imprint of Capstone
1710 Roe Crest Drive, North Mankato, Minnesota 56003
capstonepub.com

Library of Congress Cataloging-in-Publication Data is available on the Library of Congress website.

ISBN: 9798875254086 (hardcover)
ISBN: 9798875254031 (paperback)
ISBN: 9798875254048 (ebook PDF)

Summary: Artificial intelligence has already changed the world, but what's next? In this cutting-edge look at AI's future, explore the latest advancements and the exciting possibilities ahead for this technology. Will AI-powered cars make roads safer? Could AI doctors diagnose diseases before symptoms even appear? How might AI impact jobs, creativity, and the way people live? With attention-grabbing images, real-world stories, and engaging text, this book invites young readers to explore the next frontier of AI!

Editorial Credits:
Editor: Donald Lemke; Designer: Bobbie Nuytten; Media Researcher: Svetlana Zhurkin; Production Specialist: Whitney Schaefer

Image Credits:
Associated Press: File/Seth Wenig, 11; Dreamstime: Przemyslaw Ceglarek, 21; Getty Images: gremlin, 20, peepo, 4, piranka, 6, svetikd, 27, Tippapatt, 12; Newscom: UPI Photo Service/Ezio Petersen, 10; Shutterstock: Anggalih Prasetya, 5, Artsiom P, 22, Best-Backgrounds (computer code), cover and throughout, bigshot01, 14, Fabio Principe, 9, Gorodenkoff, cover (middle), 23, 24, 25, LightField Studios, 16, Mongta Studio, 19, Monkey Business Images, 26, Scharfsinn, 13, SeventyFour, 7, 29, SkillUp, cover (top) and throughout, Summit Art Creations, 15, Tada Images, 8, Toa55, 18, TY Lim, 17, Who is Danny, 28

Printed and bound in China. PO 6459

Table of Contents

CHAPTER 1

What Is AI?

Imagine a world where cars drive themselves, robots clean your room, and computers help plan your day. Sounds like something out of science fiction, right? But thanks to artificial intelligence—AI for short—these ideas are quickly becoming real.

So, what is AI? AI is when machines or computers are designed to think, learn, and make decisions like people do. You use your brain to solve problems. AI uses computer programs and data to do the same. It's like giving machines a kind of brain, so they can help us work, play, learn, and solve problems.

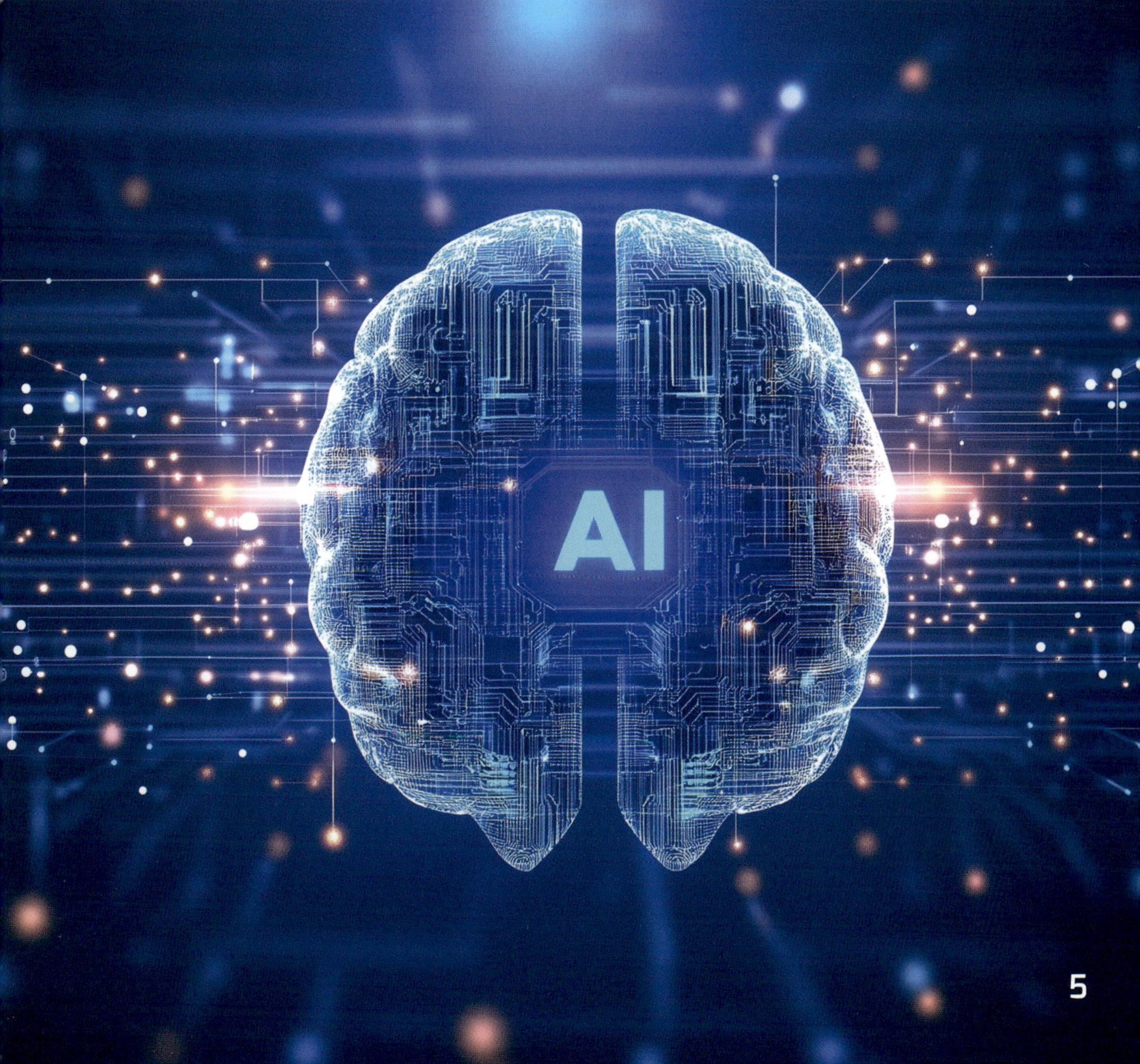

In the future, humans and AI-powered machines will work side by side to make life easier and safer.

AI is already doing amazing things. This smart technology helps doctors find the right medicines for sick patients. It helps farmers plant and harvest crops. AI even helps scientists make new discoveries.

Did You Know?

AI powers speech-to-text tools, like Google Voice Typing and Apple's Dictation. These tools listen to your voice and turn your words into written text—perfect for writing stories or taking notes.

AI is also improving the lives of people with disabilities. Some AI tools turn speech into text to help people who are deaf or hard of hearing. Other AI technology helps people who are blind or visually impaired move around safely and confidently.

AI is even being used in space! It helps astronauts explore distant planets and stars. And this is just the beginning. . . . AI is becoming a bigger part of our own world every day.

CHAPTER 2

How Has AI Changed the World?

The idea of AI began many years ago, but only recently has it become powerful enough to change the world. Some people even call AI the "brain" of the future.

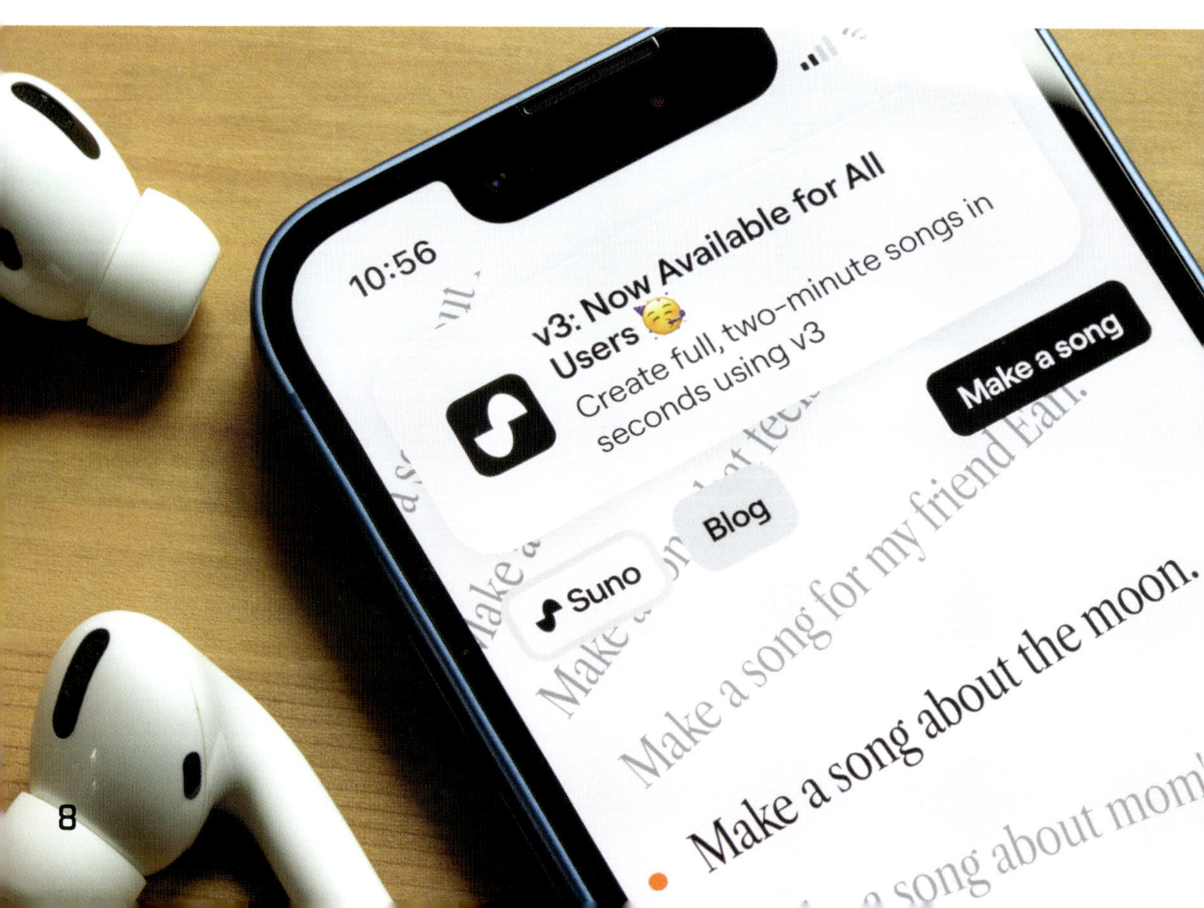

AI learns by collecting and analyzing lots of information. It's a bit like how you get better at math or reading. The more you practice, the more you understand. The more data AI receives, the smarter it becomes.

The very first AI programs were simple. They could play games like chess or solve basic puzzles. But today, AI can recognize faces, understand speech, drive cars, and even create music or stories—all at the same time! And it keeps getting better. We've only just begun to see what AI can do.

AI got its start by mastering human games. In 1997, a computer named Deep Blue shocked everyone by defeating world chess champion Garry Kasparov. It wasn't just a win—it was a wake-up call. A machine could now think strategically, plan moves ahead, and outsmart one of the best human players alive.

Did You Know?

During the match between Deep Blue and Garry Kasparov, the computer could evaluate 200 million chess moves per second! Kasparov won the first game, but Deep Blue came back to win the match.

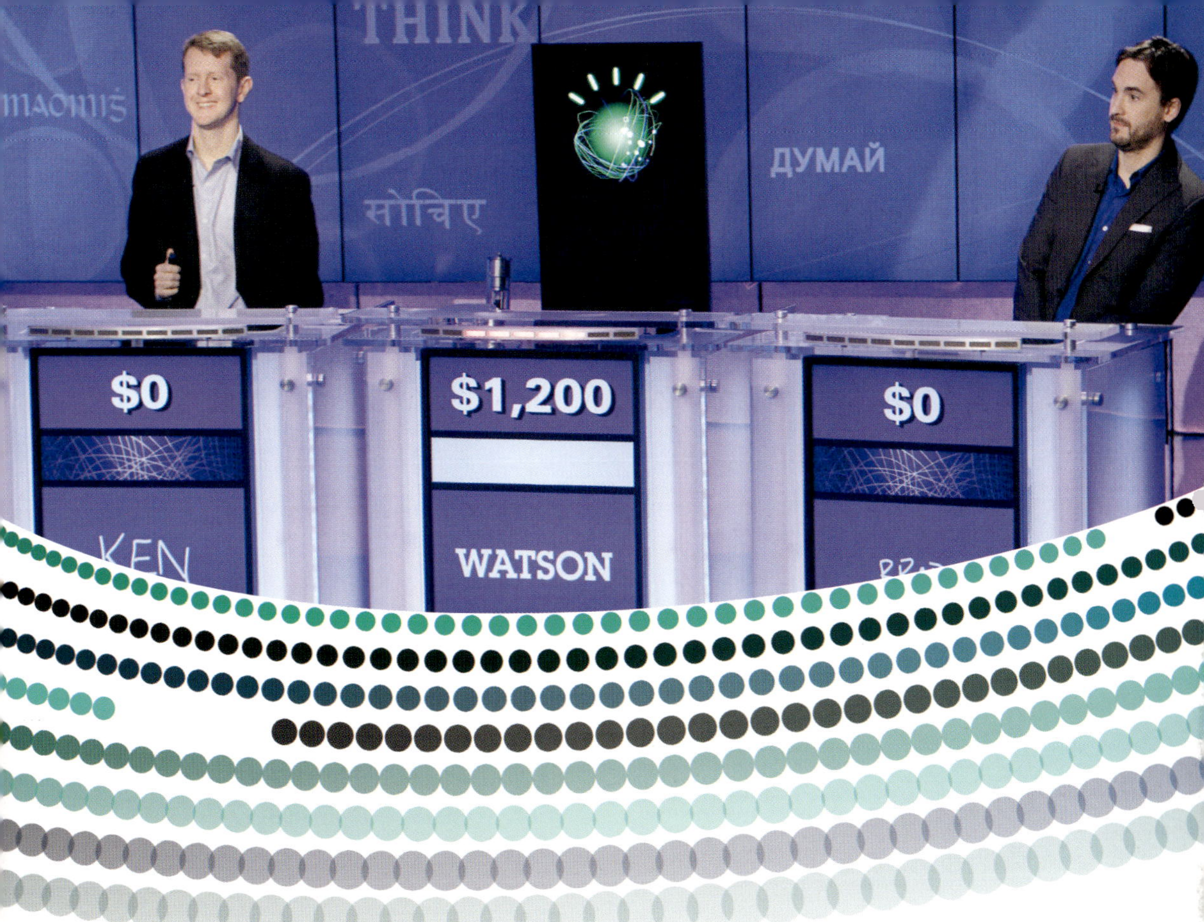

Then in 2011, IBM's AI system called Watson took on the game show *Jeopardy!*—and won big. Facing off against two of the smartest human champions, Watson read and understood thousands of books and articles in just seconds. It proved that AI could process tons of information fast and answer tough questions with lightning speed.

These game-changing moments showed that AI wasn't just smart—it was ready to take on real challenges.

One big breakthrough in AI came with something called AlexNet. In 2012, this program learned how to recognize images. It could tell the difference between a cat, a dog, and even an elephant! Soon, AI could spot differences between all kinds of images. Thanks to AI tools like AlexNet, computers can now help doctors find signs of disease in X-rays. They also help photographers organize thousands of pictures.

Did You Know?

Scientists at Stanford developed Evo 2. This AI program can analyze DNA samples. DNA makes the building blocks inside the cells of all living things. AI's analysis can predict when diseases like cancer might happen.

Another exciting leap happened with the invention of self-driving cars. These cars use AI to "see" the world around them. With the help of cameras and sensors, these vehicles can spot traffic lights, other vehicles, and even people crossing the street. AI helps the car decide when to stop, go, turn, or slow down—just like a real driver would.

CHAPTER 3

What's Next for AI?

In the next five to ten years, AI will keep getting better at doing things. Self-driving cars will become even more common. From city streets to your home, it will make everyday life easier, smarter, and safer.

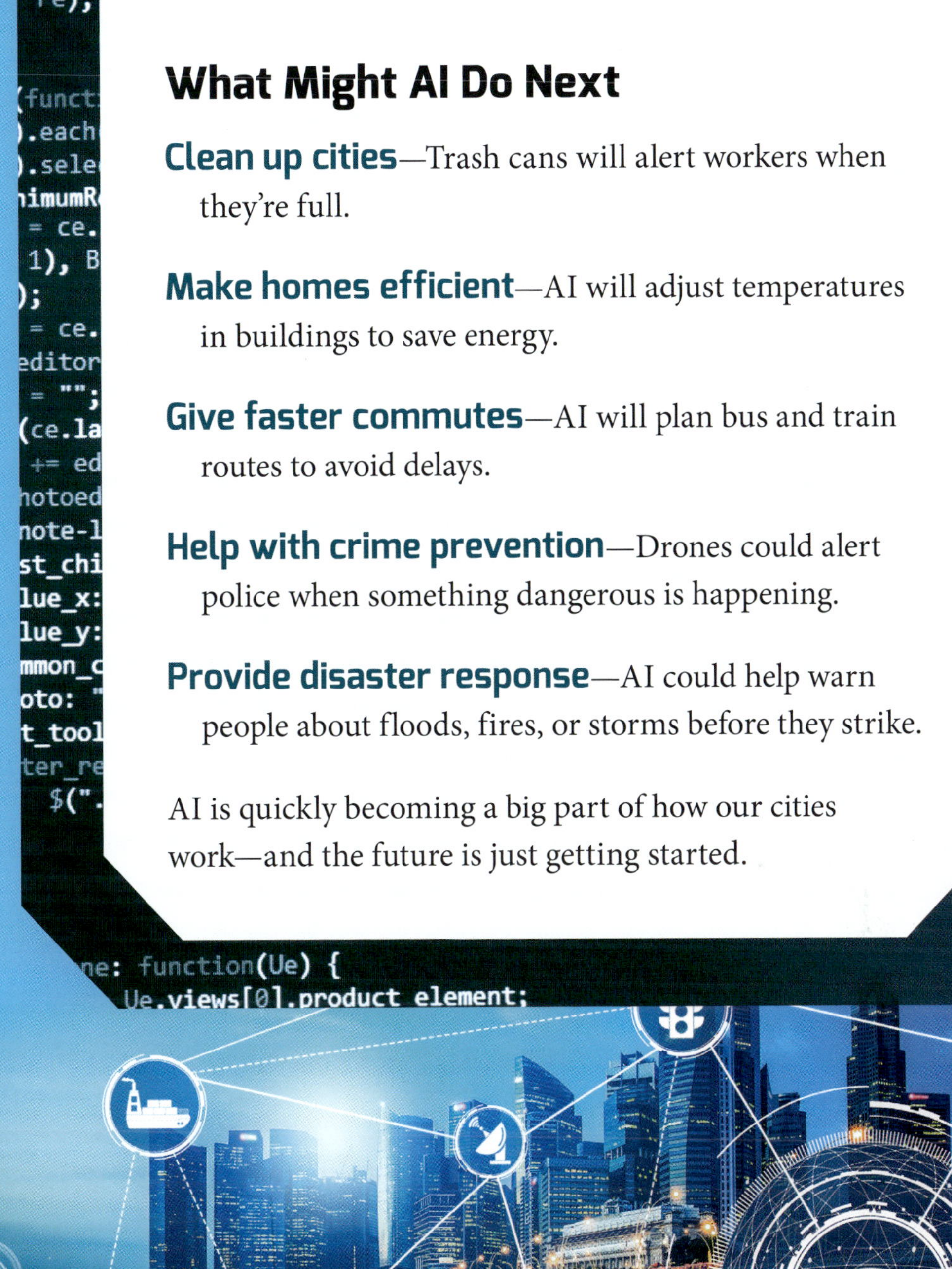

What Might AI Do Next

Clean up cities—Trash cans will alert workers when they're full.

Make homes efficient—AI will adjust temperatures in buildings to save energy.

Give faster commutes—AI will plan bus and train routes to avoid delays.

Help with crime prevention—Drones could alert police when something dangerous is happening.

Provide disaster response—AI could help warn people about floods, fires, or storms before they strike.

AI is quickly becoming a big part of how our cities work—and the future is just getting started.

AI will also help make learning more fun. AI can create virtual reality (VR) experiences in classrooms. Students can do science experiments using VR. They can travel to historical places guided by AI. A chip in your brain could transfer your thoughts to another language! Your phone's speaker could speak your thoughts in a different language to help you communicate.

Did You Know?

Medical students at University of California at San Francisco (UCSF) use VR to learn about the body. AI helps them perform lifelike surgeries.

AI could also help you stay organized. It might plan your day, remind you about appointments, or suggest fun activities based on your interests. Feeling creative? AI can help you write songs or stories—or even turn your ideas into art!

CHAPTER 4

AI Tomorrow

In the future, AI could play a big role in helping protect our planet. It will reduce pollution, save energy, and care for nature in ways never seen before.

AI-powered sensors will monitor the air, water, and soil. These sensors can detect pollution early and send warnings to people so they can take action before things get worse.

AI will also help protect forests. Drones and robots powered by AI can fly over trees to check for signs of illegal logging or wildfires. If a problem is spotted, AI can alert experts right away.

AI is already being used to fight climate change. It can help scientists predict weather patterns, track dangerous storms, and find better ways to reduce carbon dioxide in the air. AI can also suggest smart ways to use renewable energy, like wind and solar power, to help save the planet.

Did You Know?

AI models require a lot of energy to create and maintain. While they can help improve the environment, they could increase carbon emissions by 80 percent.

Much of the ocean remains unexplored because it's too deep or dangerous for humans. But AI-powered robots and submarines can dive into these unknown areas, sending back data about sea life, underwater volcanoes, and deep-sea habitats. AI helps these machines recognize different fish species, track their movements, and even spot endangered creatures.

AI can also help clean the oceans. Special robots use AI to find trash, collect it, and even sort it into recycling piles—especially harmful plastic waste that endangers sea animals. With AI's help, we can better understand and care for our oceans.

More Ways AI Could Help Planet Earth

Watching Glaciers and Ice Caps—AI can analyze satellite images to track ice in the Arctic and Antarctic.

Protecting Endangered Animals—AI-powered drones and cameras can spot rare animals in the wild, even in hard-to-reach places.

Predicting Natural Disasters—AI can study weather patterns and underground movements to warn us about hurricanes, floods, or earthquakes before they happen.

Growing Food More Sustainably—AI tools can help farmers know the best times to plant and water crops, saving water and reducing waste.

Designing Green Cities—AI can recommend materials that use less energy and designs that use sunlight or wind to power buildings—making cities cleaner and more energy efficient.

AI can do things that are too dangerous or difficult for humans. That's why AI-powered robots—like Mars rovers—are sent to explore planets. In the future, these robots could travel to even more distant worlds. They'll take pictures, collect samples, and search for signs of life—tasks that would be hard or impossible for humans to do. These robots can also learn from their surroundings and adapt to new challenges, like navigating rocky ground or storms.

Astronauts could also rely on AI to help them choose safe landing spots, repair equipment, or learn about the space around them during missions.

Back on Earth, AI is helping scientists study space too. Telescopes collect huge amounts of data about stars, planets, and galaxies. It would take humans years to sort through it all—but AI can do it in a fraction of the time! It might even help scientists discover new planets, find black holes, or learn more about how the universe began.

Did You Know?

AI can send signals nearly as fast as the speed of light. It processes data 125,000 times faster than a human brain.

CHAPTER 5

AI and Work

AI is changing the way people work—and it's just getting started. Some jobs will be done by machines, like robots that help build cars or perform quick calculations. This doesn't mean all people will lose their jobs. In fact, AI could help some workers do their jobs faster, easier, and better.

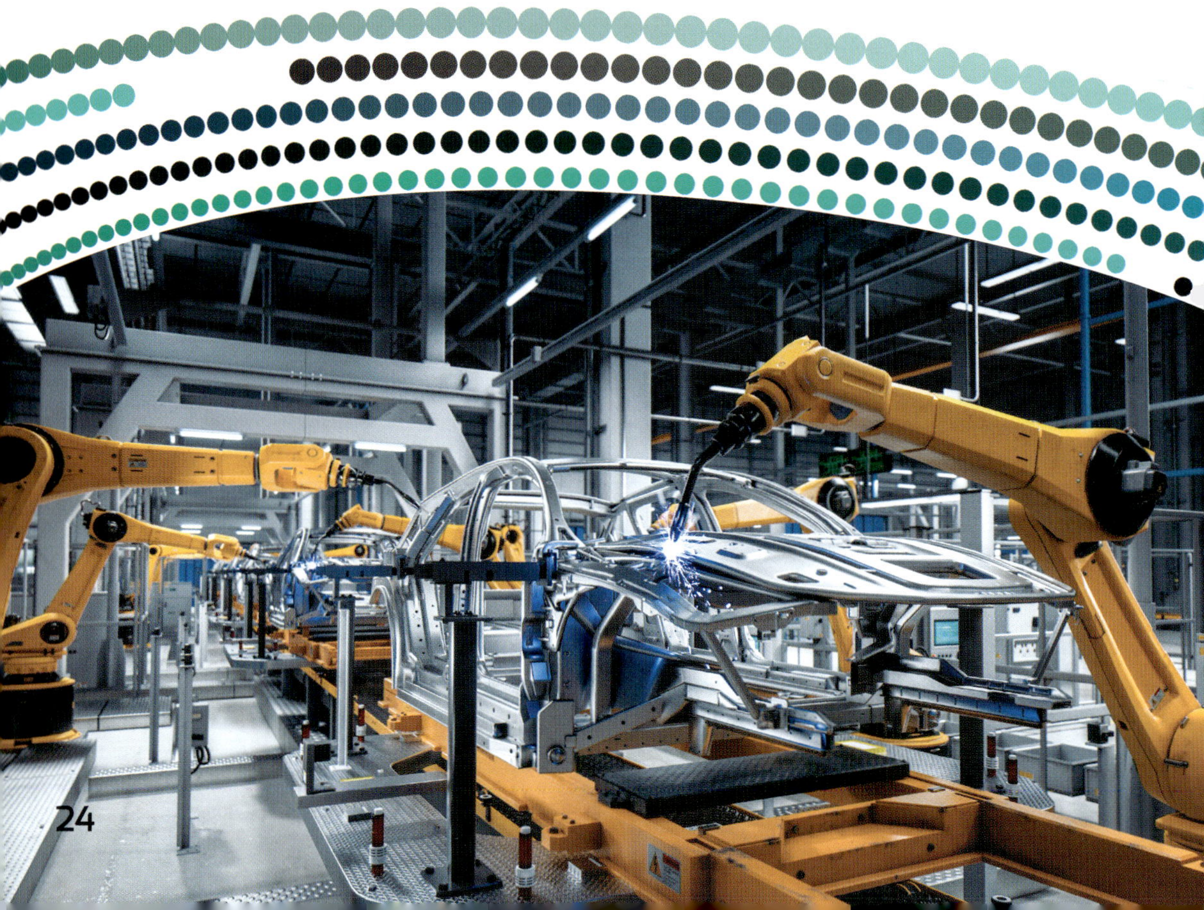

For example, robots are being used to pick fruits and vegetables in large fields. They can work quickly and carefully, helping farmers harvest food. In offices, AI can help organize files, write simple reports, and schedule meetings. This technology gives workers more time to focus on big ideas and problem-solving.

While some jobs may change, new ones will also be created. People will be needed to design, program, and repair AI tools. Jobs like AI engineer, robot technician, and data analyst are already in high demand.

So, how can you prepare for these future jobs? One way is to start learning about technology and computers. If you love solving puzzles and figuring out how things work, you're already thinking like an engineer! You can even start learning how to code. Code is the language that computers use to understand what we want them to do.

The more you learn about technology, the more exciting opportunities you'll have in the future. You could become a scientist, a robot designer, or even an AI expert.

Did You Know?

Experts predict AI to affect 300 million jobs worldwide by 2030.

Even though AI is amazing, it has some challenges. One big challenge is privacy. As AI gets smarter, it can learn a lot about us, like where we live or what we like to do. It's important to make sure that our information is kept safe, so that AI doesn't use it in ways we don't want.

Another challenge is bias. Sometimes, AI can make decisions that are unfair to certain people. For example, AI might decide that one person is better suited for a job than another. But it might be making that decision based on things like skin color or where a person comes from. It's important to teach AI to be fair to everyone.

By learning about technology, you can help shape how AI will be used in the future. Imagine creating your own robot, building an AI program, or coming up with an idea that helps people all over the world! It all starts with asking questions and staying curious.

Key AI Search Terms

1. AI for Kids
2. Artificial Intelligence Education
3. AI Learning Tools
4. AI in School
5. AI for Social Media Safety
6. AI and Privacy for Children
7. AI and Online Safety

Internet Sites

Britannica Kids: Artificial Intelligence
kids.britannica.com/kids/article/artificial-intelligence/390648

Code.org: Explore Learning for Ages 5 to 11
code.org/en-US/students/elementary

ISTE: Artificial Intelligence in Education
iste.org/ai

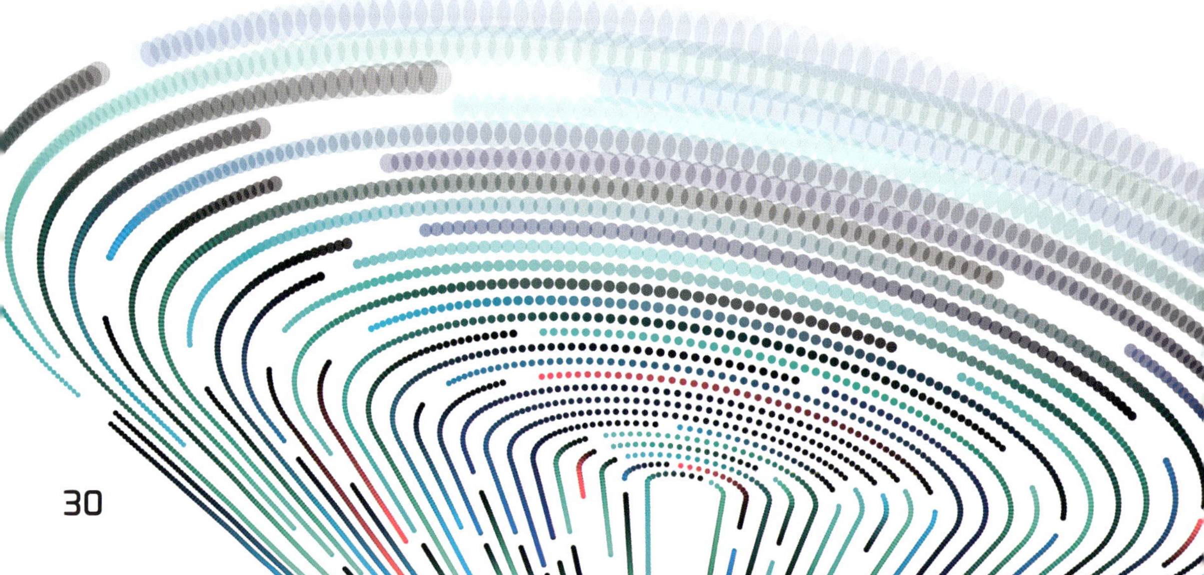

Glossary

artificial intelligence (ar-tuh-FISH-ul in-TEL-uh-jens)—when computers or machines are designed to think, learn, and solve problems like humans

bias (BY-us)—when a person or computer makes an unfair choice, often without meaning to, because of certain beliefs or limited information

climate change (KLY-mit chaynj)—long-term changes in the Earth's weather patterns, often caused by pollution or human activity

data (DAY-tuh)—information that computers use to learn and make decisions

privacy (PRY-vuh-see)—the ability to keep personal information safe and share it only when you choose

renewable energy (ri-NOO-uh-bul EN-er-jee)—energy that comes from natural sources like the sun or wind, which won't run out

virtual reality (VER-choo-uhl ree-AL-uh-tee)—a computer-created world that you can explore and interact with, like being inside a video game

Index

About the Author

Tammy Enz holds a bachelor's degree in civil engineering and a master's degree in journalism and mass communications. She works as a structural engineer and teaches at the University of Wisconsin-Platteville. She has written dozens of books on science and engineering topics for young people.